PRAYERS & PROMISES
for
Kids

BroadStreet
KIDS

CONTENTS

Introduction

It is a wonderful blessing to be a child of God! You can take great comfort in knowing that God made each child special and he wants a relationship with every one of them. Reading even just a little bit of God's Word each day puts joy in our hearts and fills us with hope.

Prayers & Promises for Kids is a topically organized collection of God's promises that guide children through lessons of confidence, love, joy, wisdom, courage, and more. Heartfelt prayers and prompting questions give kids an opportunity to think more deeply about the promises found in God's Word.

Let the children come to Jesus and be encouraged as they learn more about the love he has for them!

Belief

To all who believed him and accepted him,
he gave the right to become children of God.

JOHN 1:12 NLT

The message as it has been taught can be trusted.
He must hold firmly to it. Then he will be able to use true
teaching to comfort others and build them up. He will be
able to prove that people who oppose it are wrong.

TITUS 1:9 NIRV

Dear Jesus, thank you for dying for me. I believe in you and want to live for you every day. Help me to learn as much as I can about you in case I ever need to defend your name.

When did you start believing in Jesus?

Helpfulness

"In everything I did, I showed you that by this kind of hard work we must help the weak, remembering the words the Lord Jesus himself said: 'It is more blessed to give than to receive.'"

ACTS 20:35 NIV

"Who is more important? Is it the one at the table, or the one who serves? Isn't it the one who is at the table? But I am among you as one who serves."

LUKE 22:27 NIRV

Share with God's people who need help.
Bring strangers in need into your homes.

ROMANS 12:13 NCV

Dear Jesus, it feels good to receive help and gifts, but you say it is better to serve others instead. That is a good reminder. I want to love and help people who have less than I do.

What is something helpful you could do for someone today?

Courage

Be strong in the Lord and in his mighty power. Put on the full armor of God, so that you can take your stand against the devil's schemes.

EPHESIANS 6:10-11 NIV

Be alert. Continue strong in the faith.
Have courage, and be strong. Do everything in love.

1 CORINTHIANS 16:13-14 NCV

Even though I walk through the darkest valley,
I will not be afraid. You are with me.
Your shepherd's rod and staff comfort me.

PSALM 23:4 NIRV

"This is my command—be strong and courageous!
Do not be afraid or discouraged.
For the LORD your God is with you wherever you go."

JOSHUA 1:9 NLT

Dear God, you commanded me to always have courage. With you, I will not be discouraged or afraid. Thank you for being with me wherever I go.

When was the last time you showed courage?

Gentleness

"Accept my teachings and learn from me,
because I am gentle and humble in spirit,
and you will find rest for your lives."

MATTHEW 11:29 NCV

"Blessed are those who are humble.
They will be given the earth."

MATTHEW 5:5 NIRV

A gentle answer turns away wrath,
but a harsh word stirs up anger.

PROVERBS 15:1 NIV

Some people have gone astray without knowing it.
He is able to deal gently with them.
He can do that because he himself is weak.

HEBREWS 5:2 NIRV

Dear God, I admire how gentle you are with me. I want to treat others with the same gentleness. It's true that arguments go much more peacefully when answers are gentle instead of angry. Help me to remember that.

What are some steps you can take to become more gentle?

Obedience

Children, obey your parents in everything,
for this pleases the Lord.

COLOSSIANS 3:20 NIV

Even children are known by their behavior;
their actions show if they are innocent and good.

PROVERBS 20:11 NCV

Those who keep commandments keep their lives.
But those who don't care how they live will die.

PROVERBS 19:16 NIRV

Remember, it is sin to know what you ought to do
and then not do it.

JAMES 4:17 NLT

Dear God, sometimes I know what I should do, but I don't do it. And sometimes I know what I shouldn't do and I do it anyway. That is disobedience, and I don't want to act that way. Help me to obey my parents and you.

Why is it important to be obedient?

Prayer

LORD, in the morning you hear my voice.
In the morning I pray to you.
I wait for you in hope.

PSALM 5:3 NIRV

Never stop praying.

1 THESSALONIANS 5:17 NIRV

The Lord does not listen to the wicked,
but he hears the prayers of those who do right.

PROVERBS 15:29 NCV

Come, let us bow down in worship,
let us kneel before the LORD our Maker.

PSALM 95:6 NIV

Dear God, sometimes I don't talk to you as much as I should. You want to hear from me when good and bad things happen in my life. Help me to never stop praying. Thank you for hearing me whenever I speak.

What can you pray about right now?

Wisdom

Wisdom will come into your mind,
and knowledge will be pleasing to you.
Good sense will protect you;
understanding will guard you
It will keep you from the wicked,
from those whose words are bad.

Wisdom and money can get you almost anything,
but only wisdom can save your life.

ECCLESIASTES 7:12 NLT

If any of you needs wisdom, you should ask God for it.
He will give it to you. God gives freely to everyone
and doesn't find fault.

JAMES 1:5 NIRV

Dear God, I hear adults talk about being wise and having wisdom. It's not something I thought I could have. But you say you will give it to me if I ask for it. I want more wisdom so I can live better for you.

How could wisdom help you make better choices?

Determination

In a race all the runners run. But only one gets the prize.
You know that, don't you? So run in a way that will get you
the prize. All who take part in the games train hard. They
do it to get a crown that will not last. But we do it to get a
crown that will last forever.

1 Corinthians 9:24-25 NIRV

I have tried hard to find you—
don't let me wander from your commands.

Psalm 119:10 NLT

I have fought the good fight, I have finished the race,
I have kept the faith.

2 Timothy 4:7 NCV

Dear God, you want me to keep trying with everything
I have to finish the race and win the prize. I want to win
because living forever in heaven with you is my prize. Help me
to make it to the finish line with you.

How does winning for
God make you feel?

Boldness

He proclaimed the kingdom of God
and taught about the Lord Jesus Christ—
with all boldness and without hindrance!

ACTS 28:31 NIV

Sinners run away even when no one is chasing them.
But those who do what is right are as bold as lions.

PROVERBS 28:1 NIRV

On the day I called you, you answered me.
You made me strong and brave.

PSALM 138:3 NCV

So let us come boldly to the throne of our gracious God.
There we will receive his mercy, and we will find grace to
help us when we need it most.

HEBREWS 4:16 NLT

Dear God, sometimes I want to be quiet and not noticed, but you want me to be bold! Since you have given me strength and confidence, I pray that you will help me tell my friends about you boldly.

Why is it sometimes hard to be bold?

Encouragement

The Lord your God is with you;
the mighty One will save you.
He will rejoice over you.
You will rest in his love;
he will sing and be joyful about you.

ZEPHANIAH 3:17 NCV

Encourage one another daily,
as long as it is called "Today".

HEBREWS 3:13 NIV

Kind words are like honey—
sweet to the soul and healthy for the body.

PROVERBS 16:24 NLT

Be joyful. Grow to maturity. Encourage each other.
Live in harmony and peace. Then the God of love
and peace will be with you.

2 CORINTHIANS 13:11 NLT

Dear God, it is true that kind words feel good and make the day better. Thank you for that reminder. Help me to encourage my friends and family like you encourage me.

What encourages you when you feel down?

Anxiety

You will keep in perfect peace those whose minds are
steadfast, because they trust in you.

ISAIAH 26:3 NIV

"Don't let your hearts be troubled.
Trust in God, and trust also in me."

JOHN 14:1 NLT

Give all your worries to him,
because he cares about you.

1 PETER 5:7 NCV

I call out to the LORD when I'm in trouble,
and he answers me.

PSALM 120:1 NIRV

Dear God, I need to learn to trust in you more because you care about me and my troubles. I can worry about a lot of things, but I don't actually ever need to feel that way. Help me to reach out to you the next time I am worried.

What steps can you take to stop worrying and trust God more?

Honesty

Keep me from deceitful ways;
be gracious to me and teach me your law.
I have chosen the way of faithfulness;
I have set my heart on your laws.

PSALM 119:29-30 NIV

"Everything that is hidden will become clear,
and every secret thing will be made known."

LUKE 8:17 NCV

The king is pleased with words from righteous lips;
he loves those who speak honestly.

PROVERBS 16:13 NLT

We will speak the truth in love.

EPHESIANS 4:15 NIRV

Dear Jesus, I want to be like you and follow your laws. Honesty is important. Help me to always be truthful to my family and friends. Thank you for your example.

Is there anything you need to be honest about?

Goodness

Everything God created is good, and nothing is to be
rejected if it is received with thanksgiving.

1 TIMOTHY 4:4 NIV

Taste and see that the LORD is good.
Oh, the joys of those who take refuge in him!

PSALM 34:8 NLT

My brothers and sisters, I am sure that you are full of
goodness. I know that you have all the knowledge you
need and that you are able to teach each other.

ROMANS 15:14 NCV

Dear God, sometimes things are frustrating. My family bugs me, my friends don't understand, and things don't go my way. I know you created me to share your goodness with others. Help me to do that even when it's not easy.

What's hard about being good all the time?

Confidence

I can do everything through Christ,
who gives me strength.

PHILIPPIANS 4:13 NLT

Be my rock of refuge,
to which I can always go;
give the command to save me,
for you are my rock and my fortress....
You have been my hope, Sovereign LORD,
my confidence since my youth.

PSALM 71:3, 5 NIV

The LORD will be at your side.
He will keep your feet from being caught in a trap.

PROVERBS 3:26 NIRV

Dear God, I don't always feel confident enough to talk to new people or answer questions in large groups, but I know you are there for me. You give me the confidence I need. Thank you for being my strength.

Describe a time when God helped you feel more confident.

Love

Three things will last forever—faith, hope, and love—
and the greatest of these is love.

1 CORINTHIANS 13:13 NLT

LORD, you are good. You are forgiving.
You are full of love for all who call out to you.

PSALM 86:5 NIRV

Fill us with your love every morning.
Then we will sing and rejoice all our lives.

PSALM 90:14 NCV

Let love and faithfulness never leave you;
bind them around your neck,
write them on the tablet of your heart.

PROVERBS 3:3 NIV

Dear Jesus, you teach me that love is an important characteristic. You don't just love when it's easy. You love all the time. I want to use your love as an example of how to love others.

How can you share some of God's love today?

Peace

"I have told you these things, so that you can have peace
because of me. In this world you will have trouble. But be
encouraged! I have won the battle over the world."

JOHN 16:33 NIRV

The LORD gives his people strength.
The LORD blesses them with peace.

PSALM 29:11 NLT

Now may the Lord of peace himself give you peace at all
times and in every way. The Lord be with all of you.

2 THESSALONIANS 3:16 NIV

"I am leaving you with a gift—peace of mind and heart.
And the peace I give is a gift the world cannot give.
So don't be troubled or afraid."

JOHN 14:27 NLT

Dear God, I need to remember that you have given me the gift of peace. My life won't always be easy, but you say I never need to be afraid. Thank you for winning the battle for me.

When do you need to remember the peace God gives you?

Compassion

When I am with those who are weak, I share their weakness, for I want to bring the weak to Christ. Yes, I try to find common ground with everyone, doing everything I can to save some.

1 Corinthians 9:22 nlt

God, have mercy on me according to your faithful love. Because your love is so tender and kind, wipe out my lawless acts.

Psalm 51:1 nirv

Praise be to the God and Father of our Lord Jesus Christ, the Father of compassion and the God of all comfort.

2 Corinthians 1:3 niv

Dear God, thank you for being compassionate with me. It feels so good to know you want to share in my troubles. Guide me to have compassion for my friends and family, so I can show them the love you show me.

How can you be a more compassionate friend?

Family

Jesus, who makes people holy, and those who are made
holy are from the same family. So he is not ashamed to
call them his brothers and sisters.

HEBREWS 2:11 NCV

As we have opportunity, let us do good to all people,
especially to those who belong to the family of believers.

GALATIANS 6:10 NIV

So it is with Christ's body. We are many parts of one
body, and we all belong to each other.

ROMANS 12:5 NLT

Dear God, if your family is anything like mine, it's crazy but awesome. Thank you for making me part of your family so I can be surrounded by people who love you.

What do you love about the family God has put you in?

Integrity

I know, my God, that you test the heart and are pleased
with integrity. All these things I have given willingly and
with honest intent.

1 CHRONICLES 29:17 NIV

"So if you ignore the least commandment and teach others
to do the same, you will be called the least in the Kingdom
of Heaven. But anyone who obeys God's laws and teaches
them will be called great in the Kingdom of Heaven."

MATTHEW 5:19 NLT

The honest person will live in safety,
but the dishonest will be caught.

PROVERBS 10:9 NCV

Dear God, living with integrity means being honest and pure at all times. I know I am not perfect, but I know how you want me to live. Help me to be a good example of integrity to my friends and family.

Do you admire the integrity of anyone in your life?

Guidance

Guide me in your truth and teach me,
for you are God my Savior,
and my hope is in you all day long.

Psalm 25:5 NIV

Wise people can also listen and learn;
even they can find good advice in these words.

Proverbs 1:5 NCV

We can make our plans,
but the Lord determines our steps.

Proverbs 16:9 NLT

Those who are led by the Spirit of God
are children of God.

Romans 8:14 NIRV

Dear God, sometimes I want to do everything myself. I often think I know what's best for me. Help me to stop thinking that way because you are the one who should guide my steps and my life.

Is there anything God can help guide you in today?

Victory

You can prepare a horse for the day of battle.
But the power to win comes from the Lord.

PROVERBS 21:31 NIRV

For every child of God defeats this evil world,
and we achieve this victory through our faith.

1 JOHN 5:4 NLT

From the LORD comes deliverance.
May your blessing be on your people.

PSALM 3:8 NIV

My dear brothers and sisters, I love you and want to see
you. You bring me joy and make me proud of you,
so stand strong in the Lord as I have told you.

PHILIPPIANS 4:1 NCV

Dear Jesus, no matter how prepared I feel for my challenges, I will never totally be ready without you. When I win games with my friends or do well in competitions, help me remember all victories come from you.

What is the last victory you had?

Creativity

Lord, you have made many things;
with your wisdom you made them all.
The earth is full of your riches.

PSALM 104:24 NCV

We are God's masterpiece. He has created us anew in
Christ Jesus, so we can do the good things he planned
for us long ago.

EPHESIANS 2:10 NLT

The Lord has filled him with the Spirit of God.
He has filled him with wisdom, with understanding,
with knowledge and with all kinds of skill.

EXODUS 35:31 NIRV

We have different gifts,
according to the grace given to each of us.

ROMANS 12:6 NIV

Dear God, you are such a wonderful artist. You created all
the awesome colors and all the different faces in this world.
Help me to be creative and start using the gifts you've given me.

How can you use your
creativity for God?

Grace

Let the words you speak always be full of grace.
Learn how to make your words what people want to hear.
Then you will know how to answer everyone.

COLOSSIANS 4:6 NIRV

God gives us even more grace, as the Scripture says,
"God is against the proud, but he gives grace
to the humble."

JAMES 4:6 NCV

Sin is no longer your master, for you no longer live under
the requirements of the law. Instead, you live under the
freedom of God's grace.

ROMANS 6:14 NLT

Dear Jesus, your grace gave me forgiveness and love. It's what allows me stay in relationship with you. Help me to act with more grace during my days so I can live like you.

How can you use grace when you are with others?

Trust

"I am the way and the truth and the life. No one comes to
the Father except through me."

JOHN 14:6 NIRV

Those who know the LORD trust him,
because he will not leave those who come to him.

PSALM 9:10 NCV

I trust in you, LORD. I say, "You are my God."
My whole life is in your hands.
Save me from the hands of my enemies.
Save me from those who are chasing me.

PSALM 31:14-15 NIV

Yes, the LORD is for me; he will help me.
I will look in triumph at those who hate me.
It is better to take refuge in the LORD to trust in people.

PSALM 118:7-8 NLT

Dear Jesus, I know I can always trust you. You are the way to eternal life. Help me to come to you when I have questions about my faith or I am afraid of something. I need you.

How do you know you can trust God?

Generosity

Give generously to them and do so without a grudging
heart; then because of this the LORD your God will bless you
in all your work and in everything you put your hand to.

DEUTERONOMY 15:10 NIV

Each of you should give what you have decided in your
heart to give. You shouldn't give if you don't want to.
You shouldn't give because you are forced to.
God loves a cheerful giver.

2 CORINTHIANS 9:7 NIRV

If you help the poor, you are lending to the Lord—
and he will repay you!

PROVERBS 19:17 NLT

Dear God, it feels good to give to others, like when I share my food or toys. It feels even better knowing that when I help others, I am helping you! I want to be a cheerful giver. Help me to give generously.

How do you feel when you share with others?

Guilt

The LORD and King helps me. He won't let me be dishonored. So I've made up my mind to keep on serving him. I know he won't let me be put to shame.

ISAIAH 50:7 NIRV

Those who go to him for help are happy,
and they are never disgraced.

PSALM 34:5 NCV

No, dear brothers and sisters, I have not achieved it,
but I focus on this one thing: Forgetting the past
and looking forward to what lies ahead.

PHILIPPIANS 3:13 NLT

Dear Jesus, I want your forgiveness so that I don't feel guilty. Help me to admit my sins and ask for your grace. After that, you say I should forget the past and focus on the future. I need you to help me do this.

Why doesn't God want you to feel guilt and shame?

Anger

Don't get angry.
Don't be upset; it only leads to trouble.
Evil people will be sent away,
but those who trust the LORD will inherit the land.

PSALM 37:8-9 NCV

Everyone should be quick to listen, slow to speak and
slow to become angry, because human anger does not
produce the righteousness that God desires.

JAMES 1:19-20 NIV

"Don't sin by letting anger control you." Don't let the sun
go down while you are still angry,

EPHESIANS 4:26 NLT

Dear God, sometimes I feel really mad. I know it's not good to be angry, so please help me to cool my temper when I feel it getting out of control. I want to speak less and listen more, so I can honor you better.

What helps you settle down when you are angry?

Friendship

A friend loves you all the time,
and a brother helps in time of trouble.

"Greater love has no one than this: to lay down one's
life for one's friends. You are my friends if you do what
I command. I no longer call you servants, because a
servant does not know his master's business. Instead,
I have called you friends, for everything that I learned
from my Father I have made known to you."

There are "friends" who destroy each other,
but a real friend sticks closer than a brother.

"In everything, do to others
what you would want them to do to you."

Dear God, I love my friends, but I don't know if they know it. It is hard for me to show them how much they are appreciated. I pray that with you as my example, my actions will show my friends that they are a blessing.

What friend can you pray for right now?

Honor

"My Father will honor the one who serves me."

JOHN 12:26 NIV

Humble yourselves under the mighty power of God,
and at the right time he will lift you up in honor.

1 PETER 5:6 NLT

Anyone who wants to be godly and loving
finds life, success and honor.

PROVERBS 21:21 NIRV

Love each other like brothers and sisters. Give each
other more honor than you want for yourselves.

ROMANS 12:10 NCV

Dear God, you honor me and ask me to honor others. I should put them before myself in honor. Help me to be humble and kind. I want to be more like you every day.

How can you honor someone today?

Respect

Show respect for all people. Love the brothers and sisters
of God's family, respect God, honor the king.

1 PETER 2:17 NCV

Trust in your leaders. Put yourselves under their
authority. Do this, because they keep watch over you.
They know they are accountable to God for everything
they do. Do this, so that their work will be a joy. If you
make their work a heavy load, it won't do you any good.

HEBREWS 13:17 NIRV

Acknowledge those who work hard among you,
who care for you in the Lord and who admonish you.
Hold them in the highest regard in love because
of their work. Live in peace with each other.

1 THESSALONIANS 5:12-13 NIV

Dear God, sometimes I act rude or disrespectful when I disagree or don't get my way. You say to show respect for all people and to especially respect and obey my leaders, like parents and teachers. Help me to be more respectful to everyone in my life.

How can you show respect today?

Blessings

Surely, Lord, you bless those who do what is right.
Like a shield, your loving care keeps them safe.

Psalm 5:12 NIRV

Surely you have granted him unending blessings
and made him glad with the joy of your presence.

Psalm 21:6 NIV

"Even more blessed are all who hear the word of God
and put it into practice."

Luke 11:28 NLT

Give praise to the God and Father of our Lord Jesus
Christ. He has blessed us with every spiritual blessing.
Those blessings come from the heavenly world. They
belong to us because we belong to Christ. God chose us to
belong to Christ before the world was created. He chose
us to be holy and without blame in his eyes. He loved us.

Ephesians 1:3-4 NIRV

Dear God, thank you for everything you have given me.
I have a happy heart because of the friends you have put in
my life and the fun times you let me have. I pray I will use
the blessings in my life to honor you.

What gifts has God blessed you with lately?

Forgiveness

"If you forgive other people when they sin against you, your heavenly Father will also forgive you."

MATTHEW 6:14 NIV

Put up with each other. Forgive one another if you are holding something against someone. Forgive, just as the Lord forgave you.

COLOSSIANS 3:13 NIRV

God is faithful and fair. If we confess our sins, he will forgive our sins. He will forgive every wrong thing we have done. He will make us pure.

1 JOHN 1:9 NIRV

He is so rich in kindness and grace that he purchased our freedom with the blood of his Son and forgave our sins.

EPHESIANS 1:7 NLT

Dear God, it's not always easy to forgive others. Sometimes my friends are mean to me, and I don't feel like making peace. Please help me to forgive others just as you forgave me.

Who do you need to forgive today?

Hope

The LORD is good to those whose hope is in him,
to the one who seeks him.

LAMENTATIONS 3:25 NIV

Hope will never bring us shame. That's because God's
love has poured into our hearts. This happened through
the Holy Spirit, who has been given to us.

ROMANS 5:5 NIRV

The LORD's delight is in those who fear him,
those who put their hope in his unfailing love.

PSALM 147:11 NLT

Dear God, thank you for giving me hope that is alive. Jesus died for me and gave me the gift of the Holy Spirit. Help me to seek you in everything I do because I know that you will never let me down.

Knowing that God is always there for you, what can you be hopeful for?

Caring

Do not be interested only in your own life,
but be interested in the lives of others.

PHILIPPIANS 2:4 NCV

If anyone has material possessions and sees a brother or
sister in need but has no pity on them, how can the love
of God be in that person? Dear children, let us not love
with words or speech but with actions and in truth.

1 JOHN 3:17-18 NIV

"I was hungry. And you gave me something to eat. I was
thirsty. And you gave me something to drink. I was a
stranger. And you invited me in. I needed clothes. And
you gave them to me. I was sick. And you took care of me.
I was in prison. And you came to visit me. ...The King
will reply, 'What I'm about to tell you is true. Anything
you did for one of the least important of these brothers
and sisters of mine, you did for me.'"

MATTHEW 25:35-36, 40 NIRV

Dear God, I care about my family and my friends. Help me to be loving and caring like you are, and not to think only about myself.

How can you care for a friend today?

Diligence

The plans of the diligent lead to profit
as surely as haste leads to poverty.

PROVERBS 21:5 NIV

Work with enthusiasm, as though you were working
for the Lord rather than for people.

EPHESIANS 6:7 NLT

Many good things come from what people say.
And the work of their hands rewards them.

PROVERBS 12:14 NIRV

We must not become tired of doing good.
We will receive our harvest of eternal life
at the right time if we do not give up.

GALATIANS 6:9 NCV

Dear God, chores and homework are not always fun. You say to work with enthusiasm and to work as if I am working for you. Help me to be more diligent and to have a better attitude about working.

What will help you become more enthusiastic about work?

Salvation

"This is how God loved the world: He gave his one and only Son, so that everyone who believes in him will not perish but have eternal life."

JOHN 3:16 NLT

For the wages of sin is death, but the gift of God is eternal life in Christ Jesus our Lord.

ROMANS 6:23 NIV

God's grace has saved you because of your faith in Christ. Your salvation doesn't come from anything you do. It is God's gift.

EPHESIANS 2:8 NIRV

If you openly declare that Jesus is Lord and believe in your heart that God raised him from the dead, you will be saved.

ROMANS 10:9 NLT

Dear Jesus, thank you for dying on the cross for me. I know that I am a sinner, and you are the only way to eternal life in heaven. I want to give you my whole heart so that I can be with you always.

Do you know what it means to be saved?

Temptation

The temptations in your life are no different from what others experience. And God is faithful. He will not allow the temptation to be more than you can stand. When you are tempted, he will show you a way out so that you can endure.

1 Corinthians 10:13 NLT

"Watch and pray so that you will not fall into temptation. The spirit is willing, but the flesh is weak."

Matthew 26:41 NIV

I have taken your words to heart
so I would not sin against you.

Psalm 119:11 NCV

Dear God, temptations are hard to deal with for everyone, but you say you always give me a way out of the wrong choice. I pray that you help me to do the right thing.

What helps you resist temptation?

Thankfulness

I have not stopped giving thanks for you,
remembering you in my prayers.

EPHESIANS 1:16 NIV

Giving thanks is a sacrifice that truly honors me.
If you keep to my path,
I will reveal to you the salvation of God.

PSALM 50:23 NLT

Rejoice always, pray continually,
give thanks in all circumstances;
for this is God's will for you in Christ Jesus.

1 THESSALONIANS 5:16–18 NIV

Give thanks as you enter the gates of his temple.
Give praise as you enter its courtyards.
Give thanks to him and praise his name.

PSALM 100:4 NIRV

Dear God, you are so good! Thank you for this day. Thank you for my friends and family. Help me to give you thanks in all I do and say. You are the reason for all the blessings in my life.

What can you thank God for right now?

Strength

God is our refuge and strength,
an ever-present help in trouble.

PSALM 46:1-3 NIV

The Lord is faithful; he will strengthen you
and guard you from the evil one.

2 THESSALONIANS 3:3 NIRV

Don't be afraid, for I am with you.
Don't be discouraged, for I am your God.
I will strengthen you and help you.
I will hold you up with my victorious right hand.

ISAIAH 41:10 NLT

Dear God, I feel like I always have to act tough and strong even when I don't feel that way. It is nice to know it's okay to be weak around you because you give me strength. Thank you for keeping me safe.

How does Jesus make you feel stronger?

Learning

Those who get wisdom do themselves a favor,
and those who love learning will succeed.

PROVERBS 19:8 NCV

Pay attention to my wisdom;
listen carefully to my wise counsel.
Then you will show discernment,
and your lips will express what you've learned.

PROVERBS 5:1-2 NLT

Hold on to my teaching and don't let it go.
Guard it well, because it is your life.

PROVERBS 4:13 NIRV

Whatever you have learned or received or heard
from me, or seen in me—put it into practice.
And the God of peace will be with you.

PHILIPPIANS 4:9 NIV

Dear God, learning isn't always fun, but I know it is something I need to do. Help me to enjoy the learning that comes from you because it will teach me how you want me to live.

What helps you learn?

Joy

May the God of hope fill you with all joy and peace as you
trust in him, so that you may overflow with hope by the
power of the Holy Spirit.

Romans 15:13 NIV

"Go and enjoy good food and sweet drinks. Send some to
people who have none, because today is a holy day to the
Lord. Don't be sad, because the joy of the Lord will make
you strong."

Nehemiah 8:10 NCV

The Lord is my strength and shield.
I trust him with all my heart.
He helps me, and my heart is filled with joy.
I burst out in songs of thanksgiving.

Psalm 28:7 NLT

Dear God, thank you for joy. Thank you for letting me laugh with my friends and joke with my family. I am happy that I belong to you.

How does God make you joyful?

Patience

Warn those who are lazy. Encourage those who are timid.
Take tender care of those who are weak.
Be patient with everyone.

1 THESSALONIANS 5:14 NLT

Be like those who through faith and patience
will receive what God has promised.

HEBREWS 6:12 NCV

Be completely humble and gentle;
be patient, bearing with one another in love.

EPHESIANS 4:2 NIV

Anyone who is patient has great understanding.
But anyone who gets angry quickly shows
how foolish they are.

PROVERBS 14:29 NIRV

Dear God, patience is hard to practice, but you value patience over anger. I want to please you and treat others with love. When I feel like getting angry with someone, I pray that I will think of you and be patient instead.

What helps you be patient when you get frustrated?

Protection

My God is my rock. I can run to him for safety. He is
my shield and my saving strength, my defender and my
place of safety. The Lord saves me from those who want
to harm me.

2 Samuel 22:3 ncv

The Lord keeps you from all harm
and watches over your life.
The Lord keeps watch over you as you come and go,
both now and forever.

Psalm 121:7-8 nlt

The Lord is good, a refuge in times of trouble.
He cares for those who trust in him.

Nahum 1:7 niv

Dear God, I feel safe knowing you are always watching over me. I never have to fear the evil things of this world. Thank you for being my defender. Help me to think of you the next time I am afraid.

How does it make you feel to know God is always there to protect you?

Reliability

"All people are like grass. All their glory is like the flowers in the field. The grass dries up. The flowers fall to the ground. But the word of the Lord lasts forever."

1 PETER 1:24-25 NIRV

He will give eternal life to those who keep on doing good, seeking after the glory and honor and immortality that God offers.

ROMANS 2:7 NLT

You are near, LORD,
and all your commands are true.
Long ago I learned from your statutes
that you established them to last forever.

PSALM 119:151-152 NIV

Dear God, I know I can rely on you for anything. Nothing else in this world is as dependable as you. You are forever. Help me to get my strength from you every day.

What does it mean for you to be reliable?

Fear

God gave us his Spirit. And the Spirit doesn't make us
weak and fearful. Instead, the Spirit gives us power
and love. He helps us control ourselves.

2 TIMOTHY 1:7 NIRV

The LORD is my light and my salvation—
whom shall I fear?
The LORD is the stronghold of my life—
of whom shall I be afraid?

PSALM 27:1 NIV

When I am afraid, I will trust you.
I praise God for his word.
I trust God, so I am not afraid.
What can human beings do to me?

PSALM 56:3-4 NCV

Dear God, thank you for giving me a spirit of power and love. That makes me feel so safe. When I do feel afraid, help me to trust in you. With you in my life, I have no one to fear.

What fears can you give to God right now?

Freedom

Now the Lord is the Spirit, and where the Spirit
of the Lord is, there is freedom.

2 CORINTHIANS 3:17 NIV

My brothers and sisters, you were chosen to be free.
But don't use your freedom as an excuse to live under
the power of sin. Instead, serve one another in love.

GALATIANS 5:13 NIRV

"So if the Son sets you free, you are truly free."

JOHN 8:36 NLT

Dear Jesus, I know that you made me free so that I can choose to do good. But I am a sinner, which means sometimes I choose the wrong thing. I pray that you will help me live for you instead. Thank you for setting me free!

How does it feel to be free from your sin?

Excellence

Always think about what is true. Think about what is
noble, right and pure. Think about what is lovely and
worthy of respect. If anything is excellent or worthy of
praise, think about those kinds of things.

PHILIPPIANS 4:8 NIRV

Whatever you do, work at it with all your heart,
as working for the Lord.

COLOSSIANS 3:23 NIV'

The answer is, if you eat or drink, or if you do anything,
do it all for the glory of God.

1 CORINTHIANS 10:31 NCV

Dear God, you made me to be excellent and to represent you well. I should be thinking most about things that are good and right. Help me to think and act more like you.

Why do you think excellence is important to God?

Humility

"Didn't I make everything by my power? That is how all things were created," announces the Lord. "The people I value are not proud. They are sorry for the wrong things they have done. They have great respect for what I say."

<small>ISAIAH 66:2 NIRV</small>

Humble yourselves before the Lord,
and he will lift you up.

<small>JAMES 4:10 NIV</small>

Pride will ruin people,
but those who are humble will be honored.

<small>PROVERBS 29:23 NCV</small>

The LORD has told you what is good,
and this is what he requires of you:
to do what is right, to love mercy,
and to walk humbly with your God.

<small>MICAH 6:8 NLT</small>

Dear God, I don't want to be prideful, but sometimes I act that way. I want to be kind and humble toward my friends and family. I want them to see you in me. Help me to have more humility.

Can you describe a time when you showed humility instead of pride?

Purpose

You have been raised up with Christ. So think about
things that are in heaven. That is where Christ is.
He is sitting at God's right hand.

COLOSSIANS 3:1 NIRV

And we know that in all things God works for the good
of those who love him, who have been called according
to his purpose.

ROMANS 8:28 NIV

My child, pay attention to my words;
listen closely to what I say.
Don't ever forget my words;
keep them always in mind.

PROVERBS 4:20-21 NCV

Dear God, thank you that you have a great purpose for my life. Help me to walk closely with you, so I don't get distracted by other things. You want what is best for me and I trust you to show me what that is.

Can you think of what God might want you to do with your life?

Courtesy

Each of us should please our neighbors for their good, to build them up. For even Christ did not please himself but, as it is written: "The insults of those who insult you have fallen on me."

ROMANS 15:2-3 NIV

Remember to welcome strangers, because some who have done this have welcomed angels without knowing it.

HEBREWS 13:2 NCV

Remind God's people to obey rulers and authorities. Remind them to be ready to do what is good. Tell them not to speak evil things against anyone. Remind them to live in peace. They must consider the needs of others. They must always be gentle toward everyone.

TITUS 3:1-2 NIRV

Dear God, I want to build others up and make them feel good. Help me to encourage my friends and think about them before myself. I pray also that I can be kind to strangers and help whoever is in need.

Can you think of an example of how you could show courtesy to a friend?

Kindness

Instead, be kind to each other, tenderhearted, forgiving one another, just as God through Christ has forgiven you.

EPHESIANS 4:32 NLT

Kind people do themselves a favor,
but cruel people bring trouble on themselves.

PROVERBS 11:17 NCV

Do you disrespect God's great kindness and favor?
Do you disrespect God when he is patient with you?
Don't you realize that God's kindness is meant to turn
you away from your sins?

ROMANS 2:4 NIRV

Great is his love toward us,
and the faithfulness of the LORD endures forever.
Praise the LORD.

PSALM 117:2 NIV

Dear Jesus, your kindness is supposed to be an example for me to live by. It's not always easy to be kind, but that's how I can show your love to others. Help me to be more kind with my friends, family, and those who cross my path each day.

What is something kind you can do for someone today?

Reward

Remember that the Lord will give you an inheritance as your reward, and that the Master you are serving is Christ.

COLOSSIANS 3:24 NLT

"Love your enemies, do good to them, and lend to them without expecting to get anything back. Then your reward will be great, and you will be children of the Most High, because he is kind to the ungrateful and wicked."

LUKE 6:35 NIV

Without faith it is impossible to please God. Those who come to God must believe that he exists. And they must believe that he rewards those who look to him.

HEBREWS 11:6 NIRV

Dear God, it is better to do good deeds without expecting anything in return. Help me to have that kind of attitude when helping others. I look forward to the reward you have for me in heaven.

Why is the attitude of serving without expecting something back important to God?

Understanding

Understanding is like a fountain of life
to those who have it.
But foolish people are punished
for the foolish things they do.

PROVERBS 16:22 NIRV

The teaching of your word gives light,
so even the simple can understand.

PSALM 119:130 NLT

Give me understanding,
so that I may keep your law and obey it with all my heart.

PSALM 119:34 NIV

Don't act thoughtlessly,
but understand what the Lord wants you to do.

EPHESIANS 5:17 NLT

Dear God, I don't always know everything you want me to do, but I want to obey you. When I am confused and don't know where to turn, I will pray to you because I want to understand your ways and become more like you.

Is there anything you want God's help with understanding?

Justice

Do not try to punish others when they wrong you,
but wait for God to punish them with his anger.
It is written: "I will punish those who do wrong;
I will repay them," says the Lord.

ROMANS 12:19 NCV

He is the Rock. His works are perfect. All his ways are
right. He is faithful. He doesn't do anything wrong.
He is honest and fair.

DEUTERONOMY 32:4 NIRV

The LORD secures justice for the poor
and upholds the cause of the needy.

PSALM 140:12 NIV

There is joy for those who deal justly with others
and always do what is right.

PSALM 106:3 NLT

Dear God, there is not always justice in this world, and sometimes that makes me mad. People who do bad things aren't always punished, and people who do good things sometimes get in trouble. Help me let go of my anger and let you be the perfect judge.

Why is God the best judge for the world?

Faith

Through Christ you have come to trust in God. And you have placed your faith and hope in God because he raised Christ from the dead and gave him great glory.

1 Peter 1:21 nlt

"Because your faith is much too small. What I'm about to tell you is true. If you have faith as small as a mustard seed, it is enough. You can say to this mountain, 'Move from here to there.' And it will move. Nothing will be impossible for you."

Matthew 17:20 nirv

The important thing is faith—
the kind of faith that works through love.

Galatians 5:6 ncv

Faith is confidence in what we hope for and assurance about what we do not see.

Hebrews 11:1 niv

Dear God, faith is a confusing thing. It's not something I can see or touch or hear, but it is trusting you in my heart. I know Jesus died for me so I could live with you in heaven one day. Please live in my heart today, Jesus. I want you to be with me always.

What gives you faith and hope in Jesus?

Change

"Unless you change and become like little children,
you will never enter the kingdom of heaven."

MATTHEW 18:3 NIV

Look! I tell you this secret: We will not all sleep in death,
but we will all be changed.

1 CORINTHIANS 15:51 NCV

He will take our weak mortal bodies and change them
into glorious bodies like his own, using the same power
with which he will bring everything under his control.

PHILIPPIANS 3:21 NLT

Jesus Christ is the same yesterday and today and forever.

HEBREWS 13:8 NIRV

Dear God, change can be scary, like moving to a new house or going to a new school. But changing for you means being kind and generous and helpful to my friends and family. I want to make that kind of change. Thank you that you are perfect and you never change!

What kind of changes do you want to make for Jesus?

Cooperation

Make me truly happy by agreeing wholeheartedly with
each other, loving one another, and working together
with one mind and purpose.

PHILIPPIANS 2:2 NLT

Agree with one another. Don't be proud. Be willing to
be a friend of people who aren't considered important.
Don't think that you are better than others.

ROMANS 12:16 NIRV

Do not make friends with a hot-tempered person,
do not associate with one easily angered.

PROVERBS 22:24 NIV

Finally, all of you should be in agreement,
understanding each other, loving each other as family,
being kind and humble.

1 PETER 3:8 NCV

Dear God, cooperation means using others' ideas and my own to get something done. Sometimes we fight when we don't agree. I pray that you will help me to be loving and understanding, so I can work better with my friends.

Was there a time this week when you could have cooperated better?

Happiness

I will praise you, Lord, with all my heart.
I will tell all the miracles you have done.
I will be happy because of you; God Most High,
I will sing praises to your name.

PSALM 9:1-2 NCV

Lord, you alone are my inheritance, my cup of blessing.
You guard all that is mine.
The land you have given me is a pleasant land.
What a wonderful inheritance!

PSALM 16:5-6 NLT

Happiness makes a person smile,
but sadness can break a person's spirit.

PROVERBS 15:13 NCV

People should be happy and do good while they live.
I know there's nothing better for them to do than that.

ECCLESIASTES 3:12 NIRV

Dear God, I've learned that a happy heart is a thankful heart, so thank you for everything you've given me. I want to appreciate you and the life you've given me more from now on. Please help me to have a happier, more thankful attitude.

Is there anything you are especially happy about today?

Delight

When I received your words, I ate them.
They filled me with joy. My heart took delight in them.
Lord God who rules over all, I belong to you.

JEREMIAH 15:16 NIRV

"My God, I want to do what you want.
Your teachings are in my heart."

PSALM 40:8 NCV

Your laws are my treasure;
they are my heart's delight.

PSALM 119:111 NLT

"Let your light shine before others, that they may see
your good deeds and glorify your Father in heaven."

MATTHEW 5:16 NIV

Dear Jesus, you are in my heart, and that makes me happy! I can't wait to keep learning about you because the more I know, the more I love you. Thank you for being mine.

What is your favorite part about belonging to Jesus?

Help

My brothers and sisters, you will face all kinds of trouble.
When you do, think of it as pure joy. Your faith will be
tested. You know that when this happens it will produce
in you the strength to continue.

JAMES 1:2-3 NIRV

God will never forget the needy;
the hope of the afflicted will never perish.

PSALM 9:18 NIV

Take a new grip with your tired hands and strengthen
your weak knees. Mark out a straight path for your feet
so that those who are weak and lame will not fall but
become strong.

HEBREWS 12:12-14 NLT

"My grace is enough for you. When you are weak,
my power is made perfect in you."

2 CORINTHIANS 12:9 NCV

Dear God, there are things I cannot do alone, and that's how it should be. I should not rely on my own strength because I'm not strong enough to face the world without you. Thank you for helping me when I am weak.

What do you need God's help with?

Eternity

We are citizens of heaven, where the Lord Jesus Christ lives. And we are eagerly waiting for him to return as our Savior.

PHILIPPIANS 3:20 NLT

"And if I go and prepare a place for you, I will come back and take you to be with me that you also may be where I am."

JOHN 14:3 NIV

That will happen in a flash, as quickly as you can wink an eye. It will happen at the blast of the last trumpet. Then the dead will be raised to live forever. And we will be changed.

1 CORINTHIANS 15:52 NIRV

Surely your goodness and love will be with me all my life, and I will live in the house of the Lord forever.

PSALM 23:6 NCV

Dear Jesus, living forever is hard to imagine. It's kind of scary to think about sometimes. But living forever with you is exciting. Help me to understand what eternity means and how great a gift it is.

What questions do you have about eternity and heaven?

Praise

Sing to the Lord a new song,
his praise from the ends of the earth,
you who go down to the sea, and all that is in it,
you islands, and all who live in them.

Isaiah 42:10 NIV

Praise the LORD from the skies.
Praise him high above the earth.
Praise him, all you angels.
Praise him, all you armies of heaven.
Praise him, sun and moon.
Praise him, all you shining stars.
Praise him, highest heavens
and you waters above the sky.
Let them praise the LORD,
because they were created by his command.

Psalm 148:1-5 NCV

Dear God, you deserve so much more praise than I can give. Even the sun and moon cannot give you enough praise. Thank you for all the blessings you have given me, and thank you for sending your Son to die for me.

How can you show God praise?

Health

The world and its desires pass away,
but whoever does the will of God lives forever.

1 JOHN 2:17 NIV

Don't be wise in your own eyes.
Have respect for the Lord and avoid evil.
That will bring health to your body.
It will make your bones strong.

PROVERBS 3:7-8 NIRV

I will never forget your commandments,
for by them you give me life.

PSALM 119:93 NLT

A happy heart is like good medicine,
but a broken spirit drains your strength.

PROVERBS 17:22 NCV

Dear God, people get sick every day. Their bodies and their hearts can get sick, but you are a healer. I pray that I will follow you always and continue to ask you for health for myself and for those around me.

How can you make sure your body and your heart are healthy?

Quiet

There is a time to tear apart and a time to sew together.
There is a time to be silent and a time to speak.

<small>ECCLESIASTES 3:7 NCV</small>

It is good to wait quietly for salvation from the Lord.

<small>LAMENTATIONS 3:26 NLT</small>

Those who are careful about what they say keep
themselves out of trouble.

<small>PROVERBS 21:23 NIRV</small>

Tremble and do not sin;
when you are on your beds,
search your hearts and be silent.

<small>PSALM 4:4 NIV</small>

Dear God, it's easy to fill my head with noise. I like to listen to music, talk with my friends, play games, and watch movies. I need help learning to be quiet so I can hear your voice.

When was the last time you were quiet enough to listen to God?

Devotion

"Whoever wants to be my disciple must deny themselves
and take up their cross and follow me."

MATTHEW 16:24 NIV

"No servant can serve two masters. The servant will hate
one master and love the other, or will follow one master
and refuse to follow the other. You cannot serve both God
and worldly riches."

LUKE 16:13 NCV

Do your best to please God. Be a worker who doesn't need
to be ashamed. Teach the message of truth correctly.

2 TIMOTHY 2:15 NIRV

Don't copy the behavior and customs of this world, but
let God transform you into a new person by changing the
way you think. Then you will learn to know God's will for
you, which is good and pleasing and perfect.

ROMANS 12:2 NLT

*Dear Jesus, I am devoted to you. I like to do a lot of things,
but I want to think and act like you. Help me to keep my focus
on you so others can see my devotion and ask me about you.*

How can you show others
your devotion to Jesus?

Life

All praise to God, the Father of our Lord Jesus Christ.
It is by his great mercy that we have been born again,
because God raised Jesus Christ from the dead. Now we
live with great expectation.

1 Peter 1:3 NLT

That faith and that knowledge come from the hope for
life forever, which God promised to us before time
began.

Titus 1:2 NCV

"I am the way and the truth and the life. No one comes to
the Father except through me."

John 14:6 NIRV

Dear God, thank you for the life you have given me. I am so happy you are with me in my heart because I get to live forever! I pray that I will use everything you have given me to please you.

What is your favorite part of life?

Loneliness

"Teach them to obey everything that I have taught you,
and I will be with you always,
even until the end of this age."

MATTHEW 28:20 NCV

The LORD is near to all who call on him,
yes, to all who call on him in truth.

PSALM 145:18 NLT

Who can separate us from Christ's love?
Can trouble or hard times or harm or hunger?
Can nakedness or danger or war?

ROMANS 8:35 NIRV

"Be strong and courageous. Do not be afraid or terrified
because of them, for the LORD your God goes with you;
he will never leave you nor forsake you."

DEUTERONOMY 31:6 NIV

Dear God, sometimes I feel lonely, but it's nice to know I am never truly alone, even if other people are not around. I have nothing to be sad about or afraid of because you are right next to me all the time.

When do you feel lonely?

Worry

Turn your worries over to the LORD.
He will keep you going.
He will never let godly people be shaken.

PSALM 55:22 NIRV

"Who of you by worrying can add a single hour
to your life?"

LUKE 12:25 NIV

Worry weighs a person down;
an encouraging word cheers a person up.

PROVERBS 12:25 NLT

Do not worry about anything, but pray and ask God for
everything you need, always giving thanks. And God's
peace, which is so great we cannot understand it, will
keep your hearts and minds in Christ Jesus.

PHILIPPIANS 4:6-7 NCV

Dear God, I know that worrying about my problems does not help anything. You are all I need. You will never let me fall. And I thank you for that, Jesus. Will you help me to learn to trust in you with all my worries?

What worries can you hand over to God today?

Leadership

The Lord's servant must not be quarrelsome but must be
kind to everyone, able to teach, not resentful. Opponents
must be gently instructed, in the hope that God will grant
them repentance leading them to a knowledge of the truth.

2 TIMOTHY 2:24-25 NIV

Do what is good. Set an example for them in everything.
When you teach, be honest and serious.

TITUS 2:7 NIRV

Without wise leadership, a nation falls;
there is safety in having many advisers.

PROVERBS 11:14 NLT

Dear Jesus, you are my leader, and I learn from you. It is good to have leaders in my life so I can learn to be a leader too. Help me to set a good example for others by showing them honesty and love.

In what ways can you be a good leader?

Light

"I am the light of the world. Whoever follows me will never walk in darkness, but will have the light of life."

JOHN 8:12 NIV

"You are the light of the world—like a city on a hilltop that cannot be hidden. No one lights a lamp and then puts it under a basket. Instead, a lamp is placed on a stand, where it gives light to everyone in the house. In the same way, let your good deeds shine out for all to see, so that everyone will praise your heavenly Father."

MATTHEW 5:14-16 NLT

At one time you were in the dark. But now you are in the light because of what the Lord has done. Live like children of the light.

EPHESIANS 5:8 NIRV

Dear Jesus, because of you, I live in light instead of darkness. I don't want my friends to be in the dark, so I should let them see my light! Help me to be confident in sharing the good news with them.

How can you be a brighter light for Jesus?

BroadStreet Kids
Savage, Minnesota, USA

BroadStreet Kids is an imprint of
BroadStreet Publishing Group, LLC.
Broadstreetpublishing.com

Prayers & Promises for Kids
© 2018 by BroadStreet Publishing®

978-1-4245-5738-7 (faux)
978-1-4245-5739-4 (ebook)

Design by Chris Garborg | garborgdesign.com
Compiled and edited by Michelle Winger.

Printed in China.

18   19   20   21   22   23   24   7   6   5   4   3   2   1

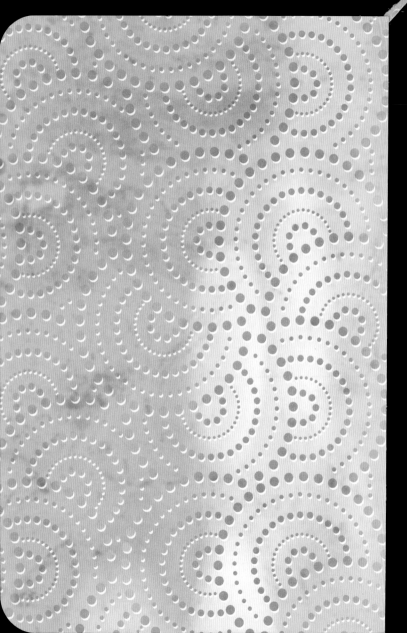